SOUL IGNITION

Volume 1

by

Crystal Williams

City of Publication: Upper Marlboro, Maryland

Printed in the United States of America

ISBN 978-1-7367236-0-9

Library of Congress Control Number: 2021903634

Soul Ignition

Written by: Crystal Williams

Editor: Exposed Books Publishing

Cover Design: Seven Pillars Design Co.

Website: www.theyoubrandacademy.com

Table of Contents

Soul Ignition

SOUL IGNITION

<u>Dedication</u>

This book is dedicated to every soul that needs encouragement throughout their career journey, business journey, and overall life journey. Always know if God gave it to you, you already have the permission to do it; therefore, it is your responsibility to do it (John 15:16)! Additionally, this book is dedicated to God, who gave me this poetic gift and allowed me to use it in a way that will uplift his people.

Introduction

I wrote these poems as I was in the midst of a career shift. Writing became very therapeutic for my soul during my journey of transitioning from my 9 to 5 corporate lifestyle to a full-time self-employment lifestyle. I had a lot of thoughts and feelings about the career transition because this was new territory for me! However, I knew that God had called me out of the auditing/accounting information technology industry to the career and professional development industry. Specifically, God instructed me to go full force within my career coaching and professional development business to position and empower individuals unhappy at work, to reclaim the authority over their career journey. In knowing those marching orders, I had to push myself and encourage myself by simply speaking life to myself, which is the root of how this book was birthed. During my writing time, God revealed that the words I was writing were not just for me. Specifically, he was telling me these poetic expressions were going to penetrate the hearts of others too. Therefore, I decided to put the poetic collections in a book and write a narrative around the poems so that others can fully understand my thought patterns at the time they were written. My thought patterns most certainly could be your thought patterns as you pursue and transition from one career to the next career or developing a prosperous business. I'm a huge advocate of having multiple streams of income outside of your 9 to 5 career, but of course, it requires courage, determination, perseverance, and another level of faith! Why, you ask? Well, it's simple because the struggles we have with our mindset can be such a distraction, and the fact of not believing in ourselves can get to us at times, and it can paralyze us from moving forward. Fortunately, the poetic expressions laid so purposely on these pages will push you and propel you to another level because they will penetrate your soul and ignite your soul! Additionally, the poetic expression aid in shifting your mindset for you to really believe you have what it takes to be all you can be. These poetic expressions are not just giving you self-confidence, it's giving you GODfidence where you are relying on God's strength more than relying on your own strength to get from Point A to Point B. It's really going to take GODfidence when you are pursuing any type of journey within your career, business, or anything you may have going on in this season of your life. I believe in you, so now is the time for YOU to believe in YOU too.

Words of Wisdom: Not sure what your divine purpose is just yet? Well, I must let you know that it's ok that you may not know what you are passionate about or what you want to do in life yet. I encourage you to pray about it, get to know YOU, and simply ask God to direct your path and send the right people across your path that will help you in your career journey, business journey, or overall life journey. To God be the glory, and I thank him in advance for your prosperous future!

<u>Soul Ignition Action Items</u>

Instructions: First Blank-Insert your name; Second Blank-Insert a career goal, business goal, or life goal to continuously remind yourself that this is the area I need the most encouragement in during this season of my life.

My name is _____, and I desire to ignite my soul to

_____

_____

_____

_____

Pray the Soul Ignition Prayer: Ignite my soul God and make me whole, especially in those areas I lack confidence. Lord, I simply ask that you strengthen my heart posture. Ignite my soul to be more in your will at all times. Guard my ear gates and my eye gates as I embark on this season of my life. Ignite my soul so I will yearn for you each and every day. Ignite my soul to yearn for your wisdom and direction, so this journey will lead me to where you want me to be and become who you want me to be. Ignite my soul as I surrender myself to you and welcome you in my heart to shape me and mold me. God, I declare and decree that you are the ultimate soul igniter, and I pray that you will be the driving force behind what I do so I can give you the glory out of my story at all times. In Jesus precious name…. Amen!

Feel free to expound upon this prayer to truly make it your own as you put your trust in God and allow him in your heart to be the ultimate soul igniter.

_____

_____

_____

_____

_____

_____

Soul Ignition Declarations:

Instructions: Recite the soul ignition declarations daily to encourage yourself. Read and reflect on the bible scriptures that align with each declaration.

I declare and decree that God is the ultimate soul igniter, and he will fill me with joy and peace as I trust in him. (Romans 15:13)

I declare and decree that I have been uniquely designed for a purpose and made in God's image. (Genesis 1:27, Psalm 139:14)

I declare and decree that my ideas are gold and given to me by God, who gives me the power to get wealth. (Deuteronomy 8:18)

I declare and decree that the work I do is not in vain, but it will build discipline, perseverance, and other characteristics needed to thrive in life. (1 Corinthians 15:58)

I declare and decree that I can do all things through Christ, who strengthens me because I believe God will give me strength when I am weary and empower me when I am weak. (Philippian 4:13, Isaiah 40:29)

Poetic Narrative

This was one of the first poems I wrote during my career transitional period. Not only did I write this poem to give notice to the world, but I wrote it to give notice to myself. Specifically, I was speaking life to myself, saying it's your time to unbox your gifts and go be great! So, I encourage you to give notice to yourself and to the world that your gifts are about to be unboxed, and this is their warning because YOU are a force to be reckoned with!

<u>GIVE NOTICE</u>

Be bold and do as you were told
By God, no matter the odds.

Give notice to the world and laugh in the face of adversity
And say "take several seats and watch me shine because
With God, I'm going to get what's mine every time."

Now be warned, the life you desire
May not happen in a Day or two,
But if you know like I know,
This is what God wants for you.

So, I thank God for your gift that was truly heaven sent,
You are the true definition of S.W.A.G.-Scholar with a Gift-
Scholar with that SWAG.

God pouring into you daily got you declaring
This will be my year of investment
That'll help me emerge into a New Testament.

Give notice to the World and never ask permission
To use your gift, God's bestowed on you, can't you see
You're on a mission?

Yes, on a mission to Do YOU.

So welcome to this peculiar part of life's journey that your
Soul been yearning to commence.

Now go, give notice, and walk-in your purpose and use
YOUR gifts that have been heaven sent.

Soul Ignition Action Items

1. Write a notification to yourself so you can look at it and remind yourself that you are on a mission, and it's your time to shine. (Example: I am notifying myself on ____(date) that I will not hesitate to be great and work in excellence to get all that God has for me. I give myself permission to live an abundant life and rebuke all my fears that may stand in my way of receiving God's promises.)

   _____

   _____

   _____

2. Reflect on your vision, write it, and attach goals to it. This will allow you to begin going after what you desire to do in your life's journey.

   _____

   _____

   _____

3. Identify what part of the poem truly ignited your soul.

_____

_____

_____

Poetic Narrative

Have you ever been sick and tired of being sick and tired?

Well, I have certainly felt that way, which is why I had to

write this poem "Refuse to Dismiss." I was sick and tired of

giving myself excuses for not using my gifts. Every excuse, I

told myself literally built monuments of nothing because

absolutely nothing I did nourish my gifts. So, one day I

simply decided that I refuse to dismiss my gifts, and I will

not continue being the world's best kept secret! Enjoy

reading this poem as I encourage you to never dismiss your

gifts.

REFUSE TO DISMISS

You see, a lot of people don't know this
But I refuse to dismiss
The gift God's bestowed on me to release to the world
The gift of poetry.

The gift to stimulate your mind
That got you saying, "Oh how kind
Of her to use her gift of words to stimulate my soul
So, I can emerge and walk into my purpose
And into that dream, that vision I see
In hopes of bringing it to reality.

So, I can begin to experience that life of prosperity."

So, just like I refused to dismiss my gift,
Never dismiss yours.

Use these words as a spiritual uplift that'll encourage your
Soul swiftly and quickly
That'll shift your mindset completely.

Your gift that'll get you thinking, "I ought to be ashamed that
I'm not using my gift to uplift
Not only me but your people, Oh God."

So, don't be afraid, push fear to the side and
Wipe them tears from your eyes and
Declare devil you are a lie.

Step out on faith and disregard the facts
No matter what may come your way
Remember, YOUR gift will lift somebody's day.

Words of Wisdom: Someone near or far is waiting for you to release your gift. Therefore, you must get excited, be bold, and release your gift to the world.

Soul Ignition Action Items

1. Repeat this: I declare and decree I will not dismiss my gift because it deserves to be released and not stay dormant within my soul.

2. What is a gift you have that you have been dismissing?

   _____

   _____

   _____

3. Make a promise to yourself to never undervalue your gifts.

4. I _____(your name) promise to never undervalue my gifts God has bestowed in me because I am God anointed and God appointed to use my gifts he has given me; therefore, it is my responsibility to use them. I am honored to be entrusted with this gift and will use it continuously to give God glory!

5. Identify what part of the poem truly ignited your soul.

_____

_____

_____

<u>Poetic Narrative</u>

It is so important to encourage yourself constantly. After all, if you don't, who will? So, take a moment right now, take out your mobile device, put it on selfie mode, and tell yourself, 'I LOVE YOU!' (P.S. don't let this be the last time you express love to yourself.)

This poetic expression was written to purely encourage myself as I go through the process of birthing the ideas God gave me. The words in this poem are literally cheering myself on and saying, be patient as I trust God to guide me through the birthing process of a dream. I encourage you to push through the birthing process, which is not easy, but it will allow you to build discipline and become more determined to be all that God wants you to be. Now go be bold and live out your dreams because the time is now. No more excuses!

THE BIRTH OF A DREAM

The year I began to invest in my passion,
My purpose, my why was 2017
The year I declared it to be 'Why Not Me?'

The year I officially stopped disqualifying myself and said,
"Oh Lord, I need you to guide me to turn my gifts and
Passions into generational wealth."

Ha! I laugh because I know that humble request would
Require work and may sometimes hurt
Which was expected because I was giving birth
To an idea God implanted in me.

Giving birth to an idea that I refuse
To let stay rent free in my mind.

Giving birth to an idea that will take
Time to come to fruition.

But I must be patient during this birthing process...
Yes, patient...yes, patient
Through the hurt, through the pain, through the agony
Of birthing a dream to reality
Just push...just keep pushing...just keep pushing!

> God's saying: I have taken you through so your Mind
> can be renewed so just keep pushing!

> Meanwhile, you're saying: But God, it's so hard, And
> I don't know about this,
> But I'll just keep pushing!

> God's saying: What the devil meant for evil, I Meant
> for good, so trust with me, you will get Through this,
> so just keep pushing!

> And you're saying: Oh Lord, I must be close Because
> the enemy is definitely out for attack, but I'll keep

pushing because I know through it all, you Always
have my back!

God's saying: The battle is not yours its mines, and
Yes, I see your daily grind, so that idea will be
Birthed in just the right time, just keep pushing!

Now that the dream is finally birthed, all I have to say is
Oh wow. This which was once a dream
Is now a reality and way better than what
I could've ever imagined it be.

This birthing process was no easy thing, but I will continue
To trust God's process over anything.

Oh God, so I know you put this idea in my head from the
Very start this year and entrusted me with everything, but
You know you're the head of my business, so together,
Let's go do this. Because I need you now more than ever.

Soul Ignition Action Items

1. What year was it that you officially declared it to be your "Why Not Me Season?" (NOTE: whatever year you declared it to be your season, cross out the 2017 and place your year there if it was not 2017.) If you have not declared it to be your "Why Not Me Season?" it is completely fine. You will one day just simply believe in yourself and trust God with everything.

   _____

   _____

   _____

2. Reflect on what ignited your soul to declare it was your season to birth your dream. If you have not declared it to be your season yet, write down what it will take for you to declare it your season to birth your dream.

   _____

   _____

   _____

3. Identify what part of the poem truly ignited your soul.

   _____

   _____

   _____

Poetic Narrative

Trusting the process should be easy, right? Well, if I'm honest, it's not easy at all! I had to really learn how to trust the process as I sought out to achieve my career goals, business goals, and life goals. Why, because I found myself becoming anxious to achieve my goals, but I quickly realized that with the type of attitude, I was beginning to idolize my goals, which is a big no, no! This poem reveals what God revealed to me about trusting the process He was taking me through. After I finished the poem, I realized that I needed to be patient and simply trust that God had me in his arms. As you read, I hope this poetic expression encourages you to trust the process God is taking you through.

<u>TRUST THE PROCESS</u>

What Would God Say To Me Right Now?

Child, I see you
But trust the process I'm taking you through.

Believe my word is true, and I got YOU.

I hear your internal screams,
And I see you're ready to embark on those dreams
That you sometimes doubt will come true.

Remember that you must go through
The storm to get the victory
And share your testimony,
So just trust ME.

Your testimony, your journey, your path is unique
That will one day inspire the weak

To get up off their feet and pursue that dream
I've bestowed on their life, to prevent them from thinking
Twice about living the life that they're meant to live.

So, trust the process, my child, I got YOU.

Just stay true to your heart,
Keep doing your thing, keep the faith, and I'll lead the way.

You can't see the victory in your life like I can,
But I never told you it would be easy
So, trust the process to the end.

What the devil meant for evil, I meant it for good, so when
You're going through and everything that's happening is a
Big ball of confusion, and you're a bit misunderstood
You're just being shaped and molded into the person that
You're meant to be but you can't see it,
So again, I say trust ME.

I got you love; I'm looking at you from heaven above.

Watching you work and make faith moves,
Watching you be a game changer in a world where
The systems that are in place are such a disgrace
And often get your mindset out of place.

YOU must stay focus,
Get what's yours, and walk in your purpose.

But you must trust ME and believe me
When I say I got you love, so trust the process.

Soul Ignition Action Items

1. Do you currently have a hard time trusting the process? If so, why?

   _____

   _____

   _____

2. What has God revealed to you about trusting the process he is taking you through?

   _____

   _____

   _____

3. Identify what part of the poem truly ignited your soul.

   _____

   _____

   _____

Poetic Narrative

Have YOU ever wavered in your faith and trust in God?

Well, I definitely have! Yes, silly, I know, but I'm just being

honest. In that moment, I had to release those thoughts

through prayer and write this poem. In this poetic expression,

I encourage you to never give up, no matter how you feel in

that moment. Additionally, this poem displays how, at times,

you may focus on the facts of your situation but focusing on

the facts will get you absolutely nowhere within your life's

journey. So simply keep the faith, trust the process, and know

that God will strengthen and empower you during your

moments of weakness.

#FAITH#TRUSTTHEPROCESS#STRENGTH

I'm a go getter, never a quitter.

I'm going to get what's mine in due time and shine
And be blessed by God who already defined
My destiny, but Lord, I pray for strength to endure the
Journey you are taking me on
Strength to endure those times where I'm like, oh come on!

The strength to celebrate each win
No matter how big or small
Each win deserves a praise,
So I must be grateful for them ALL.

I must realize, I must recognize
That your living word states that I can do ALL things
Through Christ who strengthens me, so not just one thing,
Two things, or three things
But ALL things!
But I have to believe I will achieve and receive
ALL God's blessings!

Now, back to my prayer for strength.

I pray for strength to be patient during those times where
I feel like giving up, feel like everything is in disarray
And just not going my way.

Haha lol, smiley face wink...
I'm laughing because I just said my way
But I have to remember my way is not God's way,
Whose way is always the best way
And strategically designed with me and others in mind.

Therefore, I must keep that in mind
As I travel this road called life, blind.

But trusting that God will keep me and lead me
To where he wants me in due time!

#Faith#TrustTheProcess#Strength
I pray for strength to fight off the lazy bones.
Lord, I declare, while I raise my hands in the air,
I rebuke these lazy bones.

When I talk about lazy bones,
I'm talking about struggling with procrastination,
The I know I need to do this, but it can wait, or I'll do it
Later or borderline stubborn feeling,
The waiting to the last minute feeling!

I know you've felt this way at some point in your life,
But did you also know you can have lazy bones when you
Question God's purpose for your life? Because you're
Saying really God, ME? And God's saying:
Yeah, YOU!

Why not YOU?

I've equipped you with what you
Needed since the day I created YOU!

So, don't allow the spirit of doubt,
Procrastination, and fear to appear
Heavily on your soul but declare it to disappear
And to never come near
The idea, that message, your story
That you need to pour out, and receive God's Glory!

Your life, your struggles are bigger than you, so be willing
And able to go through but know that God's got you

#Faith#TrustTheProcess#Strength...

So, if anything, I need you to remember these few things
You're a go getter, never a quitter.

Celebrate and be grateful for all wins, big or small
It's God's way, not your way, so be patient through it all.

Although not easy, don't be fearful to walk in your purpose.
Let go and let God work through you and use you
To bless others around you.

Soul Ignition Action Items

1. Reflect on a time where your faith wavered. What did you do in that moment? (Pray, write, fuss, etc.)

   _____

   _____

   _____

2. Fill in the blank: God's way is better than _____ way!

3. What characteristics, mentioned in the poem, will help you get through the waiting season?

   _____

   _____

   _____

4. Identify what part of the poem truly ignited your soul.

   _____

   _____

   _____

Poetic Narrative

Have you ever felt afraid to grow? Afraid of success? Afraid to truly become who God has called you to be? Well, I certainly have for so many reasons that ranged from not feeling qualified to letting myself and God down. As I grew closer to God and moved in faith towards my goals, I not only grew spiritually, but I also grew mentally, physically, relationally, and financially. My entire perspective on life and what I could do in life completely changed, which allowed me to unapologetically embrace my growth.

This poetic expression was birthed in the midst of my midday walk with my daughter, and I recorded my thoughts with my phone. As with any poem, I'm not only speaking to myself, but I'm speaking to you too and encouraging you to grow unapologetically and embrace the growth that is needed for you to become all that God has called you to be.

UNAPOLOGETICALLY GROWING

Growing doesn't feel good.

But you're growing, and it's showing,
You're growing, yeah YOU.

You're growing, and it's showing!
So, a round of applause for you.

A round of applause for you
For doing and pursuing what God has told you to do.

Yea it's not going to be easy,
Nope it ain't going to be easy
But it ain't meant to be easy.

Because necessary pain is the ingredients for change
Especially when you're growing, and it's showing.

It's growing, and it's showing in your character,
It's growing, and it's showing in your actions,
It's growing, and it's showing in your words,
It's growing, and it's showing in your work ethic,
You're growing, and it's showing to the world.

Yea they might not understand what you're going through
They might not understand what you're doing
But it's ok they'll get hip to it real soon.

But you know who does understand what you're doing?

God does because he told you to.

You understand who you are because of whose you are
You understand that what you're doing is not in vain,
So, the pain that you're experiencing
Is necessary for the change.

How great is our God!
How great is our God despite the odds that we face,
On a day to day basis, despite where
The journey is taking you.

Where the journey is taking you is somewhere new,
But I declare and decree that God will do
A new thing in you.

Never waiver, never give up, never give in,
You have too much that God has put within,
And it needs to just emerge,
So guess what? You got to be purged!

You got to be purged of all the iniquities,
Of all the sin, of all the doubt,
Of all the negativity that you got within you right now,
So, in a few, you'll be saying wow.

Just like that because God's got your back
And will forever have your back.

During this growing season, just seek him first.
Seek him first and continue to rehearse
What he has given to you, given to your heart
Because you're doing your part.

When you're doing your part, God will do his part.

Faith without works is dead,
And guess what? You finally got it in your head
That you are going to start and do your part.

Pause here and laugh...because you should find some joy
In this message, because that's what it is, joy.

Joy that the world can't take away
Because the world didn't give it.
Joy so deep within that's got you smiling from here to there
With such a strong grin
On your face that nobody could ever erase
Because the joy you have, they didn't give it to you,
But God did, God did that!

Man can't get no credit! Can't get none
Because what God said will be done!

NOW I must warn you that your plans may not be
The way you want it to be
But trust and believe it will be a miraculous thing.

You must realize that God is in control, and only he knows
What the future holds for you.

So, don't get discouraged, don't get dismayed
For this game of life must be played
By YOU,
The MVP, the true MVP of your life, the true MVP who
God has bestowed so much
And is just waiting for you to go, move forth,
Get on the course to do you unapologetically, of course
And be the person you were meant to be with no remorse!

Words of Wisdom: If you're not growing and showing, it's not too late to make the decision to grow and do better as an individual. Make the decision sooner rather than later because it's no time like the present.

Soul Ignition Action Items

1. Write down what you are currently doing to grow spiritually, mentally, physically, relationally, and financially?

   _____

   _____

   _____

2. What areas in action item 1 do you desire to unapologetically grow in?

   _____

   _____

   _____

3. Write down your prayer and ask God for clarity on how you can grow unapologetically in the desired areas.

_____

_____

_____

4. Identify what part of the poem truly ignited your soul.

_____

_____

_____

Poetic Narrative

Have you ever wanted to be used by God? Well, I most

certainly have wanted to be used by God, and honestly, I'm

still being used by God to elevate his Kingdom. This poem

was birthed during my season of surrender, and I was giving

God my YES to use me as his vessel. In this poem, I let God

know that I want to be a living, walking, talking witness of

what He is workin' with or, in other words, what He can truly

do to turn my situation around. I encourage you to allow God

to use you as his vessel too. I guarantee you it will be worth

it.

WHAT YOU WORKIN' WITH

Oh God, I see what you workin' with.

Oh God, only you can ignite the gifts
You have bestowed in me.

Oh God, I got to have you on my team.

Oh God, I know you're the giver of my dreams.

Oh God, I know what you workin' with,
So I'm going to stay true,
And do what you say do to make this dream come true!

Oh God, I want to show the world what you workin' with
Because only through you
Can major shifts to this world happen.

Only through you can they even begin to tap in
Their gifts and be that swift change this world needs to see.

God continue to use me, mold me, and shape me
So, I can be that beacon of light that just might,
Might? No, I will show the people of this world
What you workin' with!

I'm going to start walking in my purpose,
So, I can live in surplus,
So, I can show you how God used me to be that example to
You, to encourage you.

You too will one day start walking in your purpose
So you can live in surplus...
Wait...pause, let me talk to all of y'all, yea you who just
Doubted that statement.
Yea you living in contentment,

Who's refusing to implement
Your gifts and your talents that were meant
To be your recipe and your regiment
For an abundant life.

Yea you over there thinking twice, thinking 'that'll be nice'
But why me, God?
Wouldn't it be kind of odd for me to do that?

Meanwhile, God's tapping on you
And nagging on you and telling you
Nah, child so batter up because you're up to bat,
To bat that dream, To cast that dream, to implement that
Dream I've bestowed in you,
So, you can be a game changer and testament to the world
On what I'm workin' with.

Oh, God renew our soul and make us whole.
Stretch us wide because we're tired
Of being the world's best kept secret
And hiding our talents, our gifts, that are deep within
And only through you can they be ignited
With fuel from your fire so we know we can win.

So now I hope you see God wants to use you and me
To show the world what it is to live abundantly,
So embrace the journey.

Let go and let God, let go and let God!
Oh, God continue to use us, mold us, and shape us,
So, we can be that beacon of light that just might,
Might? No, we will show the people of this world
What YOU workin' with.

<u>Soul Ignition Action Items</u>

1. Surrender your gift(s) to God by simply giving Him your YES.

2. Reflect on how you want to be used by God to show the people of this world what God is workin' with.

   _____

   _____

   _____

3. Identify what part of the poem truly ignited your soul.

   _____

   _____

   _____

<u>Poetic Narrative</u>

Speaking life to yourself is a daily chore, or should I say a power chore you must do to empower yourself to do what it is that God has called you to do. I constantly told myself I was resilience, which is how this poem was birthed. Throughout life's journey, there will be lows, but you must be equipped with resilience to stir up your soul and get back up in this game called life.

<u>RESILIENCE</u>

Resilience, is it a part of me?

Yes, resilience is a part of me!

Resilience is a part of my DNA, it's part of my every day.

It's part of my molecular makeup that's got my soul
Saying what's UP.

You got this, so never back down from this,
This idea, this goal that's got your mind all SWOLL…
Go bounce back like never before,
Now go get that confidence to walk in your purpose to get
What God has in store.

Just give it a try, I'm not going to lie
This road ain't easy, so trust and believe me.

There will be moments
When you won't want to comment on
But did you forget that resilience is part of your DNA?

So, get up, bless up and be bold
Because your idea is GOLD!

Soul Ignition Action Items

1. Reflect on a time where you had to activate the resilience gene in your DNA.

    _____

    _____

    _____

2. Speak life to yourself by reciting this poem and ignite your soul because your idea is too golden to not be launched.

3. Identify what part of the poem truly ignited your soul.

    _____

    _____

    _____

<u>Poetic Narrative</u>

This poem was truly written in 'a moment in time.' During this moment in time, I was going through a rough week at work. I had so many deadlines to meet with very little help because my team was super small, so I was praying for God to give me the strength to make it through that moment in time. However, in the midst of it all, I had to make time to get my thoughts on paper, which is how this poem was birthed.

So, in this moment in time, I was literally ready to jump ship and just start my own business assisting individuals in landing the job of their dreams. After all, I had always dreamed of being a full-time entrepreneur, so why not now? Well, now, the beginning of 2017 was not the right time because I had literally just invested in a business coach; therefore, I was still crafting out business strategies. Additionally, I needed to build my confidence and faith muscles up because running a business was new territory to me. So, the words in this poem inspired me to hold myself accountable for meeting my goal of being a full-time entrepreneur.

The words also made me realize my career transition was going to happen sooner rather than later because I was truly being called to work in a different industry, career coaching/development. So, the fact all of this was happening to me on the job was not by coincidence. I believe it was God's way of showing me the significance of how to regain the happiness, peace, and joy in my career journey, so I truly can be the owner of my career. I'm proud to say that is exactly what I teach my clients to do in my business, The YOU Brand Academy.

A MOMENT IN TIME...

Now picture this...

I'm sitting here literally about to explode thinking about not
Being my own BOSS,
At this point, I'll do anything to fuel my passion,
No matter the COST!

Sitting here doing this type of client work
Is not what I want to do,
By the way, not having control of my life and
My schedule is driving me insane,
But what am I supposed to do?

JUMP, LEAP, STEP OUT ON FAITH you say
Okay, but I pray the Lord guides my way.

Go get it, go get it, go get it, go get your blessing
Trust God, and stop stressing!

It's my time to shine and show the world my brilliance,
My resilience to failures I may experience.

But wait ya'll I know God has me in the midst of it all,
So, when fear approaches me with all its negativity
I confront fear in its face to say, "Hello fear, yeah, I'm
Talking to you! Didn't you hear I'm confronting you?"

So now I think of fear as that hater over there
That gives me ammunition
To not depart from my mission, my vision,
And my desire to make that decision
To be my own BOSS, yes, I am the B.O.S.S.
Brilliant Optimistic Sophisticated Savvy, yeah, that's me!

I'm on a mission to do what I want to do
To make me happy,
I'm on a mission to not be complacent
But to make FAITH moves.

So, keep calm and don't be alarmed,
I'm being guided by God,
Who I know will keep me safe in his arms,
Now and forever!

But I just got to believe and know I will achieve
The blessings he has for me. Some I may only see
In a vision, for now, but not forever,
It's up to me to make those FAITH moves
So I can walk in my purpose.

Yes, I know it won't be easy,
BUT I also know you'll never leave nor forsake me
During these times of growth, which I know are necessary
To shape and mold me
Into who YOU want me to be!

So, today and every day, I say,
"YES Lord" you lead the way
I'm trusting YOU no matter what they may say.
So, in conclusion, as I close, I just want to let you know
That you are not alone.

You are NOT the only one walking around feeling like this
So, DON'T let your feelings be dismissed.

You are NOT the only one with an entrepreneurial heart.
So, go JUMP, LEAP, and START
To follow your heart to make your mark
On the world, do YOU, and be inspired by my words.

Words of Wisdom: A moment in time is just that…a moment…which means that it will not last forever and always, especially when you know God has your back forever and always.

Soul Ignition Action Items

1. Reflect on 'a moment in time' scenario you have had in your career, business, or life in general.

   _____

   _____

   _____

2. Did your moment in time ignite your soul or set you back?

   _____

   _____

   _____

3. Identify what part of the poem truly ignited your soul.

_____

_____

_____

Poetic Narrative

The spirit of fear is so paralyzing and detrimental to the soul. In the early phases of my entrepreneurial journey, I literally let fear consume me by making me think I was not good enough to do what I was called to do. Fear stopped me from going after everything God had for me. However, after a lot of prayers and cultivating a closer relationship with God, mentorship, and investment within myself and business ventures, I began to take authority over FEAR! During my quiet time, one day, the Lord instructed me to write letters to fear and rebuke it out of my life! These two poetic expressions, 'No Fear' and 'The Eviction of Fear,' are the letters I wrote to fear. I refer back to these letters when fear begins to creep up in my life in order to remind myself that I evicted the spirit of fear out of my life and refuse to be paralyzed from moving towards my career goals. I encourage you to be fearless as you pursue your career goals, business goals, and life goals.

If you find fear creeping up, simply rebuke it and do it scared. You got this!

<u>NO MORE FEAR!</u>

Silly old me wasted so much time
Being so fearful to get what's mine
To get what God has for me
That I see in my dreams.

What does fear have over me to not make dreams reality?

I quickly remembered, God did not give us the spirit of fear
So, I shout out loud, No more fear!

Fear do you hear me?

My God did not give us the spirit of fear
But of power, love, and a sound mind
So again, I shout out loud, No More Fear!

Jesus take the wheel as I confront fear…
Wipe my eyes of all the tears that have been shed here
Fear, I need you to know that you can't take away what
God has for me…
You in the way of me and my dreams.
So, you will not and cannot come looking for me,
Because I'm making my dreams a reality.
I'm pushing on, standing on faith listening to God,
So fear get out my way!

It's official, I'm shaking fear off.
It's a need to shake fear off.
You will be freed when you shake fear off.
So, despite what you think, open your eyes
And keep hope alive.

Keep the faith and don't dwell on the facts.
That's right faith over facts, so align your mind and act
Like you know, faith over facts and faith over fear
Are the fractions that are welcomed over here.

THE EVICTION OF FEAR

The Eviction of Fear in my life…
Fear you're just too much, causing me all this strife!

I declare and decree you will not be a resident in my life
So, fear you must leave because trust and believe
You are not welcome here, so get out of my ear;
You bring me no cheer
Got me out here lookin' like a deer…in head lights…
Like I don't have no direction,
But how can I have no direction
When I'm trusting in God to lead me to my destination?

So, fear you see, you must be evicted
Out of my life because I've been gifted!

Blessed by the best and doused in anointing
That is overflowing
With testimony after testimony of God's
Grace and mercy over my life!

So, fear you have no room here, your time is up!

I have too much to do, and I refuse for you
To stop me from using the gifts God's bestowed in me!

So even though I may not feel ready, I know I have all that
I need to succeed
And use my gifts in society and give God the glory!

So, I refuse to be sorry for letting you
Yeah, you fear stop me from reaching a life of prosperity
For me and my family!

So, fear this is your official EVICTION notice...
Because I'm through with YOU!

<u>Soul Ignition Action Items</u>

1. Write a letter denouncing fear in your life. When fear creeps up and prevents you from moving towards your goals, reflect on what you wrote to remind yourself that fear no longer reigns supreme in your life! You have too much to offer to the world, and life's too short to allow the spirit of fear to consume you! #ForeverFearless

   _____

   _____

   _____

2. Reflect on 2 Timothy 1:7. What does it tell you?

   _____

   _____

   _____

3. Identify what part of the poems truly ignited your soul.

   _____

   _____

   _____

<u>Poetic Narrative</u>

This poetic expression was written to uplift my brothers and sisters of color. Despite the hate, you may experience in this world due to the color of your skin, please know that your skin is not a sin. YOU are beautiful! YOU are loved by me but most importantly, by God! YOU are worthy to receive all the promises God has for you! I encourage you to always love the skin you were born in and enjoy reading this poetic expression dedicated to you.

MY SKIN IS NOT A SIN

This is dedicated to all my black people, my brown people,
And all my sisters and brothers of color,
I need to let you know that there is no OTHER!

Person like you, yeah you and your beautiful hue
Of melanin that glistens
Everywhere you go, yes,
That's right, people are going to want to know
Who you are because of the skin that wraps
Around your beautifully made body.
The skin that you should never hate but embrace,
The skin that you should never shame because it is the skin
YOU live within!

Remember, YOU are unique, one of a kind,
So don't be afraid to shine,
And do you unapologetically and show your intellectually
Critically acclaimed mind
Off to the world and let them know this:

You can try your best to oppress me, and
Knock me down because of the melanin doused in my skin,
But please trust and believe that your one-sided agenda
Will never win!

Ha! You must ain't heard that God don't play when it
Comes to his children.

So, don't come for me because of my skin
That lays so eloquently on my body
I dare you to look me in my face and tell me I'm nobody!

Ha! Well, if you accept my dare, that wouldn't be rare
But no worries because I'm blessed by the best and doused
In anointing by the one and only living God!
So, I know who I am, I know whose I am, and guess what?

MY LIFE MATTERS!
Yeah, that's right BLACK LIVES MATTER
Despite the chit chatter!

I choose to love my skin I'm in,
I choose to celebrate the skin I'm in,
Because the skin I'm in is beautiful!

I was chosen to have this skin by God, so despite the odds,
I may experience in life
Because of the skin I'm in, I choose to believe I can do
Nothing but win!

Yep my mindset is on a 110 percent, and NO, I would not
Ever think about changing the color of my skin,
It's a reminder that I got a lot of fight within
And can do nothing but WIN!

<u>Soul Ignition Action Items</u>

1. Repeat this: My skin is beautiful, and I love the skin I'm in!

2. Identify what part of the poem truly ignited your soul.

   _____

   _____

   _____

Poetic Narrative

For this poem, I had to literally reach into the future I did not

want. I literally imagined myself as an older woman who, in

my mind, I named Idle Mae. She is a lady who did not pursue

any of the ideas in her head; therefore, she was literally a

disobedient woman who did not give God her yes but

decided that an idle mind was her best. I analyzed

the mind of this woman as she recaps what an idle mind will

do to you spiritually, physically, mentally, emotionally, and

relationally. Dive deep in this poem to experience the

consequences of an idle mind but not too deep because you

never want to have an idle mind like Idle Mae.

THE COST OF AN IDLE MIND

Oohhhh, before I get too deep in the weeds
About the cost of an idle mind,
Can I just tell you that an idle mind will leave you blind!
Why? Well, it's due to the lack of vision
And always thinking you have to ask permission
Of man to be who God told you to be.

Well, if God said it, that should be enough, right?
Ha! Well, not with an idle mind.

This type of mindset will have you fearing the person
You are becoming, or should I say, could become.

Oh yes, child, an idle mind will take you off your grind.

Better yet, it will leave you grindless
And have you thinking your life is pointless,
Have you thinking your life is without purpose
And have you thinking 'it is what it is'
And who am I to do anything about it.

An idle mind will have you stuck
An a forever mood of excuses
That constantly celebrates fear instead of faith
And have you simply surviving instead of thriving
Within these detours' life throws us.

An idle mind will…Ohhh, just thinking about
An idle mind brings me to tears
Just remembering the fears, the hurt,
The pain that I eventually succumb to.

You see, that idle mind was me.
Ha! I know it's hard to believe, huh?

Well, let me explain and further break it down to you…

When your mind is fixed, it is idle.

When your mind is idle, it is missing out and full of doubt,
Always saying Am I, Am I, instead of I am, I am.

Now picture this as I paint this picture
Of what an idle mind looks like,
Imagine a brain attached to no body,
Laying in an ICU room literally, unconscious, suffocating,
Yearning to breathe, gasping for air, and slowly dying
Due to the lack of growth,
The lack of expansion in knowledge,
Knowledge that could have grown into a
Mansion of I am's!

So much potential in that idle mind
Which absolutely blows my mind
Because all I had to do was cast all my cares upon God
And move in faith and trust and believe
What God said about me,
What God whispered in my ears, here comes the tears
Which are mixed with sadness and joy
Because through it all, I'm glad I'm still here
To tell my story and give God the glory
By showing you that the cost of an idle mind
Is your purpose, your dream, your esteem,
Your blessings, your happiness,
And ultimately the promises
God gave you of a truly abundant life.

So, I encourage you today and every day
To not stand in your own way,
But to be transformed by the renewing of your mind and be
Who God has called YOU to be!

Soul Ignition Action Items

1. What does the cost of an idle mind look like to you? What will having an idle mind cost you?

    _____

    _____

    _____

2. Take what you wrote in action item 1 and develop declarations counteracting what your idle mind will cost you. For example, if you stated your idle mind will cost you 'a lifetime of regret,' your declaration will be 'I declare and decree that I will not have an idle mind that will cost me a lifetime of regret!'

    _____

    _____

    _____

3. Next, add an 'instead statement' to your declaration. For example, you can say, '…instead, I will continually move in faith to achieve my goals.' NOTE: I recommend getting specific and listing whatever goal you are seeking to achieve.

    a. The entire example declaration will read like this, 'I declare and decree that I will not have an idol mind that will cost me a lifetime of regret; instead, I will continually move in faith to achieve my goals.'

_____

_____

_____

4. Identify what part of the poem truly ignited your soul.

_____

_____

_____

Poetic Narrative

Writing this poem took me back to the first few months after my transition from one career to the next; specifically, after I voluntarily left my job to become self-employed and go full force in my business and let's just say those first few months were full of tears. Tears of joy, tears of sadness, tears of uncertainty, tears of disbelief, tears of worry, etc. Bottom line I had a lot of mixed feelings that I had to get past. It was really nothing but God's grace, mercy, and favor over my life that helped me overcome. You see, I was already in a close relationship with God, but this next chapter of life required a different level of relationship where I was literally walking around thinking 'God got me walking around saying…Yes Massa, what now?' lol no, but really because this transition into full-time self-employment was one of the biggest decisions I made because I knew it was going to be a sacrificial move and that I literally was going to be moving in faith. Absolutely no problem because I had self-confidence, but I knew that confidence in myself was great and all, but it wasn't going to be enough. Therefore, I had to elevate my self-confidence to GODfidence. What's that, you ask? Well, GODfidence is an elevated level of self-confidence where you consciously rely more on God's ability to get the job done rather than your own ability to get the job done; therefore, you're trusting and allowing God to work through you and truly strengthen you.

Have YOU ever felt like your self-confidence was not enough? If so, I encourage you to get some GODfidence because you will need it, especially in the midst of the tears and cheers experienced throughout life's journey.

<u>TEARS AND CHEERS</u>

Let's be clear these tears are real,
I mean, these things are the real deal!

Coming down my face like they are running a race,
And they're on a continuous chase
To see who can be the first to roll off my face,
By the looks of it, you would think I got sprayed
With a can of mace!

Have you been there before? Wait, I have more…
These tears running quickly out my eyes
Don't understand what it means to hide.

Why? Because they come from emotions
Full of commotion,
Full of fear, full of doubt, full of comparison,
And full of disbelief in my abilities
To truly soar to new heights I never seen before, and
Elevate to my open door season like it's a daily chore.

First, I need to get past these tears
These tears that come from a place deep within
Where my soul abodes.

The very soul that said YES to you Lord,
YES to your will, YES to your way, YES, I'll obey,
YES, I'll do whatever you say all day every day!

But why is this continuously happening when I gave you my
YES???

Is this what the YES looks like because
This is not pretty at all.

I thought my YES to you would have me standing tall,
In you, of course, but really, I just feel like
I want to curl up like a ball and give up,
But then I think about what you may say
To me in the midst of the tears:

"Giving me your yes was just the beginning, my child,
So, sit back, buckle up, and enjoy the ride.

Always look with your spiritual eyes
And not your natural eyes
Because what you are going through right now
Will only last for a while.

During this time, I need you to truly become familiar with
Who you are because of whose you are, my child, of course,
Then, and only then you will realize you are face to
Face with greatness every day
Even when you don't feel like it from day to day.

But you know these tears won't last always,
And I got your back as usual from day to day,
So simply remember YOU are VICTORIOUS and I simply
Want to use YOU to show the world what it means
To live abundantly!"

Now that was the ultimate pep talk!

So, as I dry my face by wiping my tears,
I can hear the angels yelling a cheer
"[insert name] always elevate and never negate
That what YOU have to say carries weight!"

Now that leaves me no choice but to use my voice,
And obey as God leads the way!

Soul Ignition Action Items

1. Write the type of cheer you want to hear throughout your life, career, or business journey.

   _____

   _____

   _____

   -These cheers can now be said by you in the mirror or in your phone on selfie mode, or you can simply record yourself saying the cheers and replay them when you begin to experience those tears.

2. Identify what part of the poem truly ignited your soul.

   _____

   _____

   _____

<u>Poetic Narrative</u>

Let's face it; every day, we are getting older and hopefully wiser too. But the question to ask yourself is, are YOU getting older and wiser with God? This poem was truly written as a reflection over my life, and it reveals my spiritual growth and love for God. This poem reveals the importance of the need to be in a relationship with God to truly become all you can be in this journey called life. As you build a relationship with God, who is the creator of the universe and all of mankind, you will begin to understand that you are victorious and made to win despite the ups and downs faced in life. As you build a relationship with God, you will receive the strength to boldly execute on everything that God has given you! So, I encourage you to get in a relationship with God, the ultimate soul igniter, as you get older and get wiser.

AS I GET OLDER, AS I GET WISER

As I get older, I get more bolder
As I get wiser, I know there is no other
Solution but to seek the ultimate adviser.

The one who is the true showrunner,
And the orchestrator of my life,
None other than my Lord and Savior Jesus Christ,
Who paid the ultimate sacrifice!

God, I need you always and forever
Because only you can make me better!

Only you can make me stronger,
Only you can make me whole
When my soul feels incomplete,
When my soul feels weak, when my soul feels beat,
When my soul is full of defeat,
God, it's only you I want to meet!

It's only you I trust to provide the heat
To ignite my soul and make me whole!

It's only you that can turn my situation around, and
Spark the fire beneath me to get me off the ground!

As I get older, I get more bolder
To walk out my divine mission
Because I truly know who holds the keys
To the ignition of my soul.

It becomes clearer and clearer each day I live
That I must be obedient and give
My all, tear down my walls
And relinquish control to the one who orchestrates it all.
Yes, that's right; I surrender all!

Yes, I must surrender all to the one who gave me the call,
And the one who has entrusted me with a
Special gift to uplift his people.

His sons and his daughters,
Who He wants to rain blessings down like water
From the sky because he reigns so high
Just this very fact makes me lift my hands and glorify
The one who has the true power to make a change,
The one who never loses power and
Has a signal that has a long, long range.

So, no matter how far I stray, I won't ever have to say when I
Pray, 'Can you hear me now' because God is there forever
And always and hears every heart cry I have to say!

As I get wiser,
I understand the need to know the ultimate soul igniter,
God, who gives me the strength to push through dark
Storms where He's the lighter,
That shines on my path,
So, if you mess with me, be prepared to feel His wrath
Because I'm covered, and
God don't play with His children.

As I get older,
I understand the need to be bolder
And be all God has called me to be.

After all, it's my responsibility, and it's my duty,
So never underestimate me and my abilities
To do great things because I know
Where I get my strength from,
So technically, like my Father says, it's already done!

<u>Soul Ignition Action Items</u>

1. As you get older and as you get wiser, how has God ignited your soul?

   _____

   _____

   _____

2. What are you believing God for as you get older and wiser? Do you believe it's already done?

   _____

   _____

   _____

3. Identify what part of the poem truly ignited your soul.

   _____

   _____

   _____

Poetic Narrative

Did you know laughing is good for the soul? Well, if you didn't know, I'm here to tell you that YES laughing is not only good for the soul, but it is essential for the soul! Laughing is an action that can get you through the challenges or adversities you face through your career journey, business journey, or overall life journey. With knowing and focusing on this very fact, the poem "Laugh In The Face Of Adversity" was birthed! Adversity is nothing but the enemy hindering you from being all you are called to be. This poetic expression rebukes adversity, and all it may bring within your life's journey. So, don't let adversity intimidate you; instead, simply laugh at it and push through it because you roll with God, who is the ultimate supplier of peace, joy, and happiness.

LAUGH IN THE FACE OF ADVERSITY

I laugh in the face of adversity
Because I know the majority
Of the time it ain't nothing but the enemy
Who must don't know with God I already got the victory!

Trying to steal my joy by jumping my spirit,
Kill my soul by making me think with God I'm not whole,
And demolishing my mind to take me off my grind
Simply wasting my time by distracting me,
Trying to tell me not to believe in me
By getting in my head and, saying that dream is dead, and
Saying all those tears, you shed are worthless and pointless'
And after a while, the enemy's words sound like
Blah blah blah blah blah and
Finally, I say, oh, nah!

Enemy, you will not snatch me down to the ground, and
Try to take away my crown that is rightfully mines
You must have forgotten I'm a child of the king,
So I've got Royalty
In my blood running all throughout my body.

So, I know, despite what I hear, think, or sometimes speak,
"I KNOW I AM SOMEBODY!"

Somebody destined to be great
Somebody destined to win
Somebody destined to live in
Spiritual, mental, physical, financial,
And relational abundance!

But I know with anything it's going to take sacrifice
That's always got me thinking twice
About going after what God wants or
Should I say has called me to be.

But not anymore because I refuse to adore
Those negative thoughts
Yeah, those thoughts from you know who,
Whose tricks get old
Always selling me pipe dreams,
But fortunately for me, I don't fall for those schemes
Because my life is already sold to the ultimate dream team
God the Father, the Son, & the Holy Spirit!

So, I refuse to entertain those thoughts and get distracted
Because my mind, body, and soul are so connected
To the true source that empowers me and never devours me
So, as I stay in my divine lane and do what I do with God, I
Declare and decree that 'my work is Not in vain
And the enemy will not manipulate my brain!'

So, with my head held high,
I continue to walk out this journey called life,
Live in victory and laugh in the face of adversity!

Soul Ignition Action Items:

1. Fill in the blank: Laughing is _____ for the soul!

2. What current situation are you facing that you need to laugh at to help you overcome? Whatever the situation is, speak life to it and declare you are victorious! Please know that the battles or adversities you face are the Lord's and not yours; therefore, give all your burdens to God, who is equipped to handle every single one of them.

   _____

   _____

   _____

3. Take a picture of you laughing and place it on your vision/declaration board. It will symbolize you are laughing in the face of adversity and remind you that you will get through it because God is on your side.

4. Identify what part of the poem truly ignited your soul.

   _____

   _____

   _____

INSPIRATIONAL QUOTES

These quotes are my top 20 quotes I love to use to inspire, empower, and position individual's mindset to reach the next level within their 9 to 5 career journey, business journey, or overall life's journey! Overall, my goal is to impact your soul so you can thrive and not just survive through life. Feel free to put these quotes on your workstation, vision board, or turn them into declarations!

"Celebrating mini-wins is a necessity to maintain your sanity throughout life's journey."

"Following 'the crowd' will get you nowhere, but following God will get you everywhere."

"Refuel, recharge, and relax your body; you only get one, so treat it right so you can be the light God needs you to be."

"Don't expect for anyone else to invest in YOU before YOU invest in yourself."

"Don't let the spirit of comparison kill the person you're truly meant to be!"

"Don't expect anyone else to nurture the person you see in the mirror if YOU don't even nurture yourself."

"Being stagnant is not an option for you, as a matter of fact, it's not even a part of the ingredients that embody you!"

"Don't let perfectionism get in the way of your productivity!"

"Life's too short to abort your dream, so go forth, execute, and live out your dream."

"Dwelling on past mistakes is a waste of time, instead take authority over your situation by using your time wisely to press forward!"

"Never undervalue the gift God has bestowed in YOU!"

"Believe that YOU were made to WIN!"

"Every good fruit that your life produces are because of God's amazing grace and favor over you."

"Success looks different to everyone; therefore, don't allow anyone to define your definition of success in your life!"

"You are an unboxed individual that is on a mission to die empty of all what God has given you to elevate His people."

"Never be ashamed or afraid to invest in yourself to get the help you may need to LEVEL UP! Remember, getting help is not a sign of weakness, but it's a sign of maturity which takes strength."

"Expecting man to come through for you is foolish, but expecting God to come through for you is wise."

"Be in the business of the 'DO' and not the business of the 'HOW' because that's God's job."

"Simply make the CHOICE to be great and doing what you need to do to ELEVATE, you are worth it!"

"Don't be afraid to carry your calling, if God called YOU to it, He will carry YOU through it."

CPSIA information can be obtained
at www.ICGtesting.com
Printed in the USA
LVHW051437060621
689465LV00006B/133

9 781736 723609